# 50 Vanilla Cooking Recipes

By: Kelly Johnson

# Table of Contents

- Vanilla Bean Panna Cotta
- Vanilla Glazed Carrots
- Vanilla Roasted Sweet Potatoes
- Vanilla Infused Mashed Potatoes
- Vanilla Chicken with Honey Glaze
- Vanilla Poached Pears
- Vanilla Bean Ice Cream
- Vanilla Almond Granola
- Vanilla French Toast
- Vanilla Yogurt Parfait
- Vanilla Cream Scones
- Vanilla Buttermilk Pancakes
- Vanilla Chia Pudding
- Vanilla Rice Pudding
- Vanilla Cupcakes
- Vanilla Bean Cheesecake
- Vanilla Custard

- Vanilla Poppy Seed Muffins
- Vanilla Bean Donuts
- Vanilla Apple Crisp
- Vanilla Bread Pudding
- Vanilla Marshmallows
- Vanilla Glazed Salmon
- Vanilla Pork Tenderloin
- Vanilla Infused Balsamic Vinaigrette
- Vanilla Bean Shortbread
- Vanilla Caramel Sauce
- Vanilla Cream Pie
- Vanilla Milkshake
- Vanilla Bean Hot Chocolate
- Vanilla Spice Rubbed Chicken
- Vanilla Cauliflower Purée
- Vanilla Bean Crème Brûlée
- Vanilla Bean Waffles
- Vanilla Macarons
- Vanilla Roasted Nuts

- Vanilla Orange Glazed Chicken
- Vanilla Maple Glazed Brussels Sprouts
- Vanilla Eggnog
- Vanilla Ice Cream Sandwiches
- Vanilla Bean Biscotti
- Vanilla Almond Butter
- Vanilla Maple Roasted Squash
- Vanilla Coconut Pudding
- Vanilla Oatmeal with Berries
- Vanilla Infused Olive Oil
- Vanilla Peach Cobbler
- Vanilla Lemon Bars
- Vanilla Hazelnut Spread
- Vanilla Glazed Donut Holes

**Vanilla Bean Panna Cotta**
**Ingredients:**

- 2 cups heavy cream
- ½ cup whole milk
- ½ cup sugar
- 1 vanilla bean (split and scraped)
- 2½ tsp gelatin
- 3 tbsp cold water

**Instructions:**
Sprinkle gelatin over cold water.
Heat cream, milk, sugar, and vanilla in a saucepan until steaming.
Remove from heat, stir in gelatin until dissolved.
Pour into ramekins and chill 4–6 hours.

**Vanilla Glazed Carrots**

**Ingredients:**

- 1 lb baby carrots
- 2 tbsp butter
- 1 tbsp honey
- ½ tsp vanilla extract
- Salt to taste

**Instructions:**
Steam or boil carrots until tender.
Melt butter in a pan, add honey and vanilla.
Toss carrots in glaze until coated and glossy.

**Vanilla Roasted Sweet Potatoes**

**Ingredients:**

- 2 large sweet potatoes, cubed
- 2 tbsp olive oil
- 1 tbsp maple syrup
- ½ tsp vanilla extract
- Salt and cinnamon to taste

**Instructions:**

Toss sweet potatoes with oil, maple syrup, vanilla, salt, and cinnamon. Roast at 400°F (200°C) for 25–30 minutes, turning halfway.

**Vanilla Infused Mashed Potatoes**
**Ingredients:**

- 2 lbs potatoes, peeled and boiled
- ½ cup milk
- ¼ cup butter
- ¼ tsp vanilla extract
- Salt and pepper to taste

**Instructions:**
Mash potatoes with warm milk and butter.
Stir in vanilla, season, and blend until smooth.

**Vanilla Chicken with Honey Glaze**
**Ingredients:**

- 4 boneless chicken breasts
- Salt and pepper
- 1 tbsp olive oil
- 2 tbsp honey
- 1 tsp vanilla extract
- 1 tbsp soy sauce

**Instructions:**
Season and sear chicken in oil.
Mix honey, vanilla, and soy sauce, then pour over chicken.
Simmer until cooked through and glazed.

**Vanilla Poached Pears**

**Ingredients:**

- 4 firm pears, peeled
- 2 cups water
- 1 cup sugar
- 1 vanilla bean (split and scraped)
- Optional: splash of white wine

**Instructions:**
Simmer water, sugar, and vanilla until dissolved.
Add pears and simmer until tender, about 20 minutes.
Serve with syrup.

**Vanilla Bean Ice Cream**
**Ingredients:**

- 2 cups heavy cream
- 1 cup whole milk
- ¾ cup sugar
- 1 vanilla bean (split and scraped)
- 5 egg yolks

**Instructions:**
Heat milk, cream, sugar, and vanilla.
Whisk hot liquid into egg yolks, return to pan, and cook until thickened.
Chill mixture, then churn in an ice cream maker.

**Vanilla Almond Granola**

**Ingredients:**

- 3 cups rolled oats
- 1 cup sliced almonds
- ½ cup honey
- ¼ cup coconut oil
- 1 tsp vanilla extract

**Instructions:**

Mix oats and almonds.
Warm honey, oil, and vanilla, then stir into oat mixture.
Bake at 325°F (160°C) for 20–25 minutes, stirring halfway.

**Vanilla French Toast**
**Ingredients:**

- 4 slices thick bread
- 2 eggs
- ½ cup milk
- 1 tsp vanilla extract
- 1 tsp cinnamon
- Butter for pan

**Instructions:**
Whisk eggs, milk, vanilla, and cinnamon.
Dip bread and cook in a buttered skillet until golden on both sides.
Serve with syrup or powdered sugar.

**Vanilla Yogurt Parfait**
**Ingredients:**

- 2 cups vanilla yogurt
- 1 cup granola
- 1 cup fresh berries

**Instructions:**
Layer yogurt, granola, and berries in glasses or jars.
Repeat layers and serve chilled.

**Vanilla Cream Scones**
 **Ingredients:**

- 2 cups flour
- ¼ cup sugar
- 1 tbsp baking powder
- ½ tsp salt
- ½ cup butter (cold, cubed)
- ½ cup heavy cream
- 1 egg
- 1 tsp vanilla extract

**Instructions:**
Mix dry ingredients. Cut in butter until crumbly.
Whisk cream, egg, and vanilla, then combine with flour mixture.
Form into a circle, cut into wedges, and bake at 400°F (200°C) for 15–18 minutes.

**Vanilla Buttermilk Pancakes**

**Ingredients:**

- 1½ cups flour
- 2 tbsp sugar
- 1 tsp baking powder
- ½ tsp baking soda
- ¼ tsp salt
- 1 egg
- 1 cup buttermilk
- 2 tbsp melted butter
- 1 tsp vanilla extract

**Instructions:**
Combine dry ingredients. In another bowl, mix wet ingredients.
Stir together until just combined.
Cook on a greased griddle until golden.

**Vanilla Chia Pudding**

**Ingredients:**

- 2 cups milk (or non-dairy)
- ½ cup chia seeds
- 2 tbsp maple syrup or honey
- 1 tsp vanilla extract

**Instructions:**
Mix all ingredients well.
Refrigerate for 4+ hours or overnight, stirring once early on.
Top with fruit if desired.

**Vanilla Rice Pudding**

**Ingredients:**

- ½ cup white rice
- 2 cups milk
- ¼ cup sugar
- ½ tsp vanilla extract
- Pinch of salt

**Instructions:**

Simmer rice in milk with sugar and salt until soft and creamy. Stir in vanilla and serve warm or chilled.

**Vanilla Cupcakes**

**Ingredients:**

- 1½ cups flour
- 1½ tsp baking powder
- ¼ tsp salt
- ½ cup butter
- ¾ cup sugar
- 2 eggs
- 1 tsp vanilla extract
- ½ cup milk

**Instructions:**

Cream butter and sugar, beat in eggs and vanilla.
Alternate adding dry ingredients and milk.
Bake at 350°F (175°C) for 18–20 minutes.

**Vanilla Bean Cheesecake**

**Crust:**

- 1½ cups graham cracker crumbs
- ¼ cup melted butter

**Filling:**

- 3 (8 oz) packages cream cheese
- ¾ cup sugar
- Seeds from 1 vanilla bean
- 1 tsp vanilla extract
- 3 eggs

**Instructions:**
Press crust into pan and bake at 325°F (160°C) for 10 minutes.
Beat filling ingredients and pour over crust.
Bake for 45–50 minutes. Chill before serving.

**Vanilla Custard**
**Ingredients:**

- 2 cups whole milk
- ¼ cup sugar
- 4 large egg yolks
- 1 vanilla bean (split and scraped) or 1 tsp vanilla extract
- 1 tbsp cornstarch
- Pinch of salt

**Instructions:**
Heat milk, sugar, and vanilla in a saucepan.
Whisk egg yolks, cornstarch, and salt in a bowl.
Slowly pour warm milk into the egg mixture, then return to the pan and cook over low heat until thickened.
Cool and serve chilled.

**Vanilla Poppy Seed Muffins**
**Ingredients:**

- 1½ cups flour
- ½ cup sugar
- 1 tsp baking powder
- ¼ tsp baking soda
- ½ tsp salt
- 2 tbsp poppy seeds
- 1 egg
- 1 cup buttermilk
- ¼ cup butter (melted)
- 1 tsp vanilla extract

**Instructions:**
Combine dry ingredients, then stir in poppy seeds.
In another bowl, whisk wet ingredients.
Mix both together and fill muffin cups.
Bake at 350°F (175°C) for 18–20 minutes.

**Vanilla Bean Donuts**

**Ingredients:**

- 2 cups flour
- 1 tsp baking powder
- ½ tsp baking soda
- ¼ tsp salt
- ½ cup sugar
- 1 egg
- 1 cup buttermilk
- 1 tsp vanilla extract
- ½ tsp vanilla bean seeds
- ¼ cup melted butter

**Instructions:**
Mix dry ingredients, then add wet ingredients.
Spoon batter into a donut pan and bake at 375°F (190°C) for 12–15 minutes.
Cool and glaze with a vanilla glaze if desired.

**Vanilla Apple Crisp**

**Ingredients:**

- 4 apples, peeled and sliced
- ½ cup sugar
- 1 tsp cinnamon
- 1 tbsp lemon juice
- 1 cup rolled oats
- ½ cup flour
- ¼ cup brown sugar
- 1/3 cup butter (cold, cubed)
- ½ tsp vanilla extract

**Instructions:**

Toss apples with sugar, cinnamon, and lemon juice, and place in a baking dish. Combine oats, flour, brown sugar, and butter, then sprinkle over apples. Bake at 350°F (175°C) for 40–45 minutes.

**Vanilla Bread Pudding**
 **Ingredients:**

- 4 cups cubed bread (preferably stale)
- 2 cups milk
- ½ cup sugar
- 3 eggs
- 1 tsp vanilla extract
- 1 tsp cinnamon
- ¼ cup butter (melted)
- ½ cup raisins (optional)

**Instructions:**
Whisk together milk, sugar, eggs, vanilla, and cinnamon.
Toss bread cubes with the milk mixture, and pour into a greased baking dish.
Bake at 350°F (175°C) for 35–40 minutes.
Serve warm with caramel sauce or whipped cream.

**Vanilla Marshmallows**

**Ingredients:**

- 1½ cups water (divided)
- 3 packets gelatin
- 1 cup sugar
- 1 cup light corn syrup
- 1 tsp vanilla extract
- Pinch of salt

**Instructions:**
Bloom gelatin in ½ cup water.
Heat sugar, corn syrup, and remaining water until boiling, then pour over gelatin.
Whisk in vanilla and salt, then pour into a greased pan and let set overnight.
Cut into squares and dust with powdered sugar.

**Vanilla Glazed Salmon**
**Ingredients:**

- 4 salmon fillets
- ¼ cup honey
- 1 tbsp soy sauce
- 1 tsp vanilla extract
- 1 tsp lemon juice
- Salt and pepper to taste

**Instructions:**
Whisk together honey, soy sauce, vanilla, and lemon juice.
Season salmon with salt and pepper, then brush with glaze.
Grill or bake at 375°F (190°C) for 12–15 minutes, basting halfway through.

**Vanilla Pork Tenderloin**

**Ingredients:**

- 1 lb pork tenderloin
- 1 tbsp olive oil
- 2 tbsp honey
- 1 tsp vanilla extract
- 1 tsp Dijon mustard
- Salt and pepper to taste

**Instructions:**
Season pork with salt and pepper.
Sear pork in olive oil over medium-high heat.
Combine honey, vanilla, mustard, and pour over pork.
Roast at 375°F (190°C) for 20–25 minutes, basting occasionally.

**Vanilla Infused Balsamic Vinaigrette**
**Ingredients:**

- ¼ cup balsamic vinegar
- ½ cup olive oil
- 1 tsp vanilla extract
- 1 tsp Dijon mustard
- 1 tbsp honey
- Salt and pepper to taste

**Instructions:**
Whisk all ingredients together until emulsified.
Serve over salads or roasted vegetables.

**Vanilla Bean Shortbread**

**Ingredients:**

- 2 cups flour
- 1 cup butter (softened)
- ½ cup powdered sugar
- 1 tsp vanilla bean seeds (or extract)
- Pinch of salt

**Instructions:**
Mix butter, sugar, and vanilla.
Gradually add flour and salt.
Chill dough for 30 minutes, then roll out and cut into shapes.
Bake at 350°F (175°C) for 10–12 minutes.

**Vanilla Caramel Sauce**
**Ingredients:**

- 1 cup sugar
- 6 tbsp butter
- ½ cup heavy cream
- 1 tsp vanilla extract
- Pinch of salt

**Instructions:**
Melt sugar over medium heat until golden.
Add butter and cream, whisking until smooth.
Stir in vanilla and salt.
Cool and drizzle over desserts.

**Vanilla Cream Pie**
**Ingredients:**

- 1 pie crust (baked)
- 2 cups milk
- 1 vanilla bean (split and scraped)
- 3 eggs
- ¾ cup sugar
- ¼ cup cornstarch
- 1 tbsp butter

**Instructions:**
Heat milk and vanilla bean in a saucepan.
Whisk eggs, sugar, and cornstarch, then slowly add the hot milk mixture.
Return to the pan and cook until thickened.
Cool, then pour into crust.
Top with whipped cream.

**Vanilla Milkshake**

**Ingredients:**

- 2 cups vanilla ice cream
- 1 cup milk
- 1 tsp vanilla extract
- Whipped cream for topping

**Instructions:**

Blend ice cream, milk, and vanilla until smooth.
Serve with whipped cream and a cherry on top.

**Vanilla Bean Hot Chocolate**

**Ingredients:**

- 2 cups milk
- 2 tbsp cocoa powder
- 2 tbsp sugar
- 1 vanilla bean (split and scraped)
- Pinch of salt
- Whipped cream (optional)

**Instructions:**

Heat milk with cocoa powder, sugar, vanilla bean, and salt.
Simmer until hot and well combined.
Serve with whipped cream.

**Vanilla Spice Rubbed Chicken**
**Ingredients:**

- 4 chicken breasts
- 1 tbsp brown sugar
- 1 tsp ground cinnamon
- 1 tsp smoked paprika
- 1 tsp vanilla extract
- Salt and pepper to taste

**Instructions:**
Mix brown sugar, cinnamon, paprika, vanilla, salt, and pepper.
Rub the mixture onto the chicken.
Grill or bake at 375°F (190°C) for 20–25 minutes.

**Vanilla Cauliflower Purée**

**Ingredients:**

- 1 head cauliflower, chopped
- 1 tbsp butter
- ½ cup heavy cream
- 1 tsp vanilla extract
- Salt and pepper to taste

**Instructions:**
Steam cauliflower until tender.
Blend with butter, cream, vanilla, salt, and pepper until smooth.
Serve as a side dish.

**Vanilla Bean Crème Brûlée**

**Ingredients:**

- 2 cups heavy cream
- 1 vanilla bean (split and scraped)
- 5 egg yolks
- ½ cup sugar
- ¼ cup brown sugar (for topping)

**Instructions:**
Heat cream and vanilla bean until simmering.
Whisk egg yolks and sugar, then slowly add the hot cream mixture.
Bake at 325°F (160°C) for 30–35 minutes.
Chill, then top with brown sugar and caramelize with a torch.

**Vanilla Bean Waffles**

**Ingredients:**

- 2 cups flour
- 1 tbsp sugar
- 1 tsp baking powder
- ¼ tsp salt
- 2 eggs
- 1½ cups milk
- 1 tsp vanilla bean seeds (or vanilla extract)
- 1/3 cup melted butter

**Instructions:**

Mix dry ingredients.
Whisk together eggs, milk, vanilla, and melted butter.
Combine both mixtures and stir gently.
Cook in a preheated waffle iron until golden.
Serve with syrup or fresh fruit.

**Vanilla Macarons**

**Ingredients:**

- 1 cup powdered sugar
- ½ cup almond flour
- 2 large egg whites
- ¼ cup sugar
- 1 tsp vanilla extract
- Pinch of salt
- Buttercream for filling (optional)

**Instructions:**

Sift almond flour and powdered sugar together.
Whisk egg whites with sugar until stiff peaks form.
Gently fold in the dry ingredients and vanilla.
Pipe onto a baking sheet and bake at 300°F (150°C) for 15-18 minutes.
Cool and fill with buttercream.

**Vanilla Roasted Nuts**

**Ingredients:**

- 2 cups mixed nuts (almonds, cashews, pecans)
- 1 tbsp vanilla extract
- 1 tbsp honey
- ½ tsp cinnamon
- Pinch of salt

**Instructions:**
Preheat oven to 350°F (175°C).
Toss nuts with vanilla, honey, cinnamon, and salt.
Spread in a single layer on a baking sheet and roast for 10-12 minutes, stirring halfway.
Cool and serve.

**Vanilla Orange Glazed Chicken**
 Ingredients:

- 4 chicken breasts
- 1 orange (juiced and zested)
- 2 tbsp honey
- 1 tsp vanilla extract
- 1 tbsp soy sauce
- Salt and pepper to taste

**Instructions:**
Combine orange juice, zest, honey, vanilla, soy sauce, salt, and pepper.
Marinate chicken for at least 30 minutes.
Grill or bake at 375°F (190°C) for 20-25 minutes, basting with the glaze.

**Vanilla Maple Glazed Brussels Sprouts**

**Ingredients:**

- 1 lb Brussels sprouts (trimmed and halved)
- 2 tbsp olive oil
- 2 tbsp maple syrup
- 1 tsp vanilla extract
- Salt and pepper to taste

**Instructions:**

Preheat oven to 400°F (200°C).
Toss Brussels sprouts with olive oil, maple syrup, vanilla, salt, and pepper.
Roast for 20-25 minutes, stirring halfway through.

**Vanilla Eggnog**

**Ingredients:**

- 2 cups milk
- 1 cup heavy cream
- 4 large egg yolks
- ½ cup sugar
- 1 tsp vanilla extract
- ¼ tsp ground nutmeg
- Pinch of salt

**Instructions:**
Heat milk and cream over medium heat.
Whisk egg yolks and sugar until pale, then slowly add the milk mixture.
Cook until thickened, then remove from heat and add vanilla, nutmeg, and salt.
Chill and serve with a sprinkle of nutmeg.

**Vanilla Ice Cream Sandwiches**

**Ingredients:**

- 2 cups vanilla ice cream (softened)
- 24 cookies (chocolate chip or oatmeal)

**Instructions:**

Scoop ice cream onto one cookie, then sandwich with another.
Freeze for 30 minutes to set.
Serve chilled.

**Vanilla Bean Biscotti**
**Ingredients:**

- 2 cups flour
- 1 cup sugar
- 1 tsp baking powder
- 1 tsp vanilla bean seeds (or vanilla extract)
- 2 large eggs
- ½ cup sliced almonds

**Instructions:**
Mix dry ingredients and add eggs and vanilla.
Shape into a log and bake at 350°F (175°C) for 20 minutes.
Slice and bake for another 10-12 minutes until crisp.

**Vanilla Almond Butter**
**Ingredients:**

- 2 cups raw almonds
- 1 tsp vanilla extract
- 1 tbsp honey
- Pinch of salt

**Instructions:**
Process almonds in a food processor until smooth.
Add vanilla, honey, and salt, and process until fully incorporated.
Store in an airtight jar.

**Vanilla Maple Roasted Squash**
**Ingredients:**

- 1 small butternut squash (peeled and cubed)
- 2 tbsp olive oil
- 2 tbsp maple syrup
- 1 tsp vanilla extract
- ½ tsp cinnamon
- Salt and pepper to taste

**Instructions:**
Preheat oven to 400°F (200°C).
Toss squash with olive oil, maple syrup, vanilla, cinnamon, salt, and pepper.
Spread on a baking sheet and roast for 25-30 minutes until tender and caramelized.

**Vanilla Coconut Pudding**

**Ingredients:**

- 1 can (14 oz) full-fat coconut milk
- ½ cup sugar
- 2 tbsp cornstarch
- 1 tsp vanilla extract
- Pinch of salt

**Instructions:**

In a saucepan, whisk together coconut milk, sugar, cornstarch, and salt.
Bring to a boil over medium heat, stirring constantly, until thickened.
Remove from heat and stir in vanilla.
Pour into bowls and refrigerate for at least 2 hours before serving.

**Vanilla Oatmeal with Berries**
**Ingredients:**

- 1 cup rolled oats
- 2 cups milk (or dairy-free milk)
- 1 tsp vanilla extract
- 1 tbsp maple syrup
- 1 cup mixed berries (strawberries, blueberries, raspberries)

**Instructions:**
Cook oats in milk according to package instructions.
Stir in vanilla and maple syrup.
Top with fresh berries and serve.

**Vanilla Infused Olive Oil**

**Ingredients:**

- 1 cup extra virgin olive oil
- 1 vanilla bean (split and scraped)

**Instructions:**

Combine olive oil and vanilla bean in a saucepan over low heat.
Let it heat gently for 5-10 minutes, then remove from heat and let cool.
Transfer to a bottle and let infuse for 2-3 days before using in salads or drizzling over dishes.

**Vanilla Peach Cobbler**
**Ingredients:**

- 4 cups fresh peaches (peeled and sliced)
- 1 tbsp lemon juice
- 1 tbsp sugar
- 1 tsp vanilla extract
- 1 cup flour
- 1 tsp baking powder
- ½ cup sugar
- 1/4 tsp salt
- ½ cup milk
- 1/4 cup butter (melted)

**Instructions:**
Preheat oven to 375°F (190°C).
Toss peaches with lemon juice, sugar, and vanilla, then place in a baking dish.
In a bowl, combine flour, baking powder, sugar, salt, milk, and butter to form a batter.
Drop spoonfuls of batter over peaches and bake for 35-40 minutes, or until golden brown.

**Vanilla Lemon Bars**
**Ingredients:**

- 1 cup flour
- ½ cup powdered sugar
- ½ cup butter (softened)
- 2 eggs
- 1 cup granulated sugar
- 1 tbsp lemon zest
- ¼ cup lemon juice
- 1 tsp vanilla extract
- ¼ cup flour

**Instructions:**
Preheat oven to 350°F (175°C).
Combine flour, powdered sugar, and butter to form the crust, then press into the bottom of a greased pan.
Bake for 15 minutes.
Whisk together eggs, granulated sugar, lemon zest, lemon juice, vanilla, and flour.
Pour over the baked crust and bake for 20 minutes until set.
Cool and dust with powdered sugar.

**Vanilla Hazelnut Spread**
**Ingredients:**

- 1 cup roasted hazelnuts (skin removed)
- 2 tbsp cocoa powder
- 1/3 cup powdered sugar
- 2 tbsp honey
- 1 tsp vanilla extract
- 2 tbsp coconut oil

**Instructions:**
Process hazelnuts in a food processor until smooth.
Add cocoa powder, sugar, honey, vanilla, and coconut oil.
Process until well combined.
Store in a jar and enjoy on toast, pancakes, or fruit.

**Vanilla Glazed Donut Holes**
**Ingredients:**

- 1 cup flour
- ¼ cup sugar
- 1 tsp baking powder
- ¼ tsp salt
- 1/3 cup milk
- 1 egg
- 2 tbsp butter (melted)
- 1 tsp vanilla extract
- 1 cup powdered sugar (for glaze)
- 2 tbsp milk (for glaze)

**Instructions:**
Preheat oil for frying in a deep pan.
Mix flour, sugar, baking powder, and salt.
Whisk together milk, egg, melted butter, and vanilla.
Combine wet and dry ingredients, then form small dough balls and fry for 2-3 minutes until golden.
Whisk powdered sugar and milk to make the glaze.
Dip donut holes in glaze and let set before serving.